To:

_____

From:

_____

Date:

_____

Trust in the Lᴏʀᴅ forever, for the Lᴏʀᴅ God
is an everlasting rock.

Isaiah 26:4

"Do not let your hearts be troubled.
You believe in God; believe also in Me."

John 14:1

The LORD gives strength to His people;
the LORD blesses His people with peace.

Psalm 29:11

Put your hope in the Lord.
Travel steadily along His path.

Psalm 37:34

"I know the plans I have for you," declares the Lord, "plans to prosper you and not to harm you, plans to give you hope and a future."

Jeremiah 29:11

Your Word is a lamp to guide my feet
and a light for my path.

Psalm 119:105

"Do not be afraid; do not be discouraged, for the LORD your God will be with you wherever you go."

Joshua 1:9

The LORD says, "I will guide you along the best pathway for your life. I will advise you and watch over you."

Psalm 32:8

Commit to the Lᴏʀᴅ whatever you do,
and He will establish your plans.

Proverbs 16:3

Whether you turn to the right or to the left,
your ears will hear a voice behind you, saying,
"This is the way; walk in it."

Isaiah 30:21

God said, "My Presence will go with you.
I'll see the journey to the end."

Exodus 33:14

God is our God for ever and ever;
He will be our Guide even to the end.

Psalm 48:14

God is our refuge and strength,
a very present help in trouble.

Psalm 46:1

Cast your cares on the LORD and He will sustain you.

Psalm 55:22

"Be still, and know that I am God."

Psalm 46:10

The LORD is good, a refuge in times of trouble.
He cares for those who trust in Him.

Nahum 1:7

The Lᴏʀᴅ Himself goes before you and will be with you;
He will never leave you nor forsake you.

Deuteronomy 31:8

We have this hope as an anchor for the soul,
firm and secure.

Hebrews 6:19

Whoever dwells in the shelter of the Most High
will rest in the shadow of the Almighty.

Psalm 91:1

The eternal God is your refuge,
and underneath are the everlasting arms.

Deuteronomy 33:27

The Lord is my rock, my fortress and my deliverer;
my God is my rock, in whom I take refuge.

Psalm 18:2

I can do everything through Christ,
who gives me strength.

Philippians 4:13

The LORD will be your confidence and
will keep your foot from being caught.

Proverbs 3:26

Blessed is the one who trusts in the LORD,
whose confidence is in Him.

Jeremiah 17:7

Trust in the LORD forever, for the LORD God
is an everlasting rock.

Isaiah 26:4

"Do not let your hearts be troubled.
You believe in God; believe also in Me."

The LORD gives strength to His people;
the LORD blesses His people with peace.

Psalm 29:11

Put your hope in the LORD.
Travel steadily along His path.

Psalm 37:34

"I know the plans I have for you," declares the LORD, "plans to prosper you and not to harm you, plans to give you hope and a future."

Jeremiah 29:11

Your Word is a lamp to guide my feet
and a light for my path.

Psalm 119:105

"Do not be afraid; do not be discouraged, for the Lᴏʀᴅ
your God will be with you wherever you go."

Joshua 1:9

The Lord says, "I will guide you along the best pathway for your life. I will advise you and watch over you."

Commit to the LORD whatever you do,
and He will establish your plans.

Proverbs 16:3

Whether you turn to the right or to the left,
your ears will hear a voice behind you, saying,
"This is the way; walk in it."

Isaiah 30:21

God said, "My Presence will go with you.
I'll see the journey to the end."

Exodus 33:14

God is our God for ever and ever;
He will be our Guide even to the end.

Psalm 48:14

God is our refuge and strength,
a very present help in trouble.

Psalm 46:1

Cast your cares on the Lord and He will sustain you.

Psalm 55:22

"Be still, and know that I am God."

Psalm 46:10

The Lᴏʀᴅ is good, a refuge in times of trouble.
He cares for those who trust in Him.

Nahum 1:7

The LORD Himself goes before you and will be with you;
He will never leave you nor forsake you.

Deuteronomy 31:8

We have this hope as an anchor for the soul,
firm and secure.

Whoever dwells in the shelter of the Most High
will rest in the shadow of the Almighty.

The eternal God is your refuge,
and underneath are the everlasting arms.

Deuteronomy 33:27

The Lᴏʀᴅ is my rock, my fortress and my deliverer;
my God is my rock, in whom I take refuge.

Psalm 18:2

I can do everything through Christ,
who gives me strength.

Philippians 4:13

The Lᴏʀᴅ will be your confidence and
will keep your foot from being caught.

Proverbs 3:26

Blessed is the one who trusts in the LORD,
whose confidence is in Him.

Jeremiah 17:7

Trust in the LORD forever, for the LORD God
is an everlasting rock.

Isaiah 26:4

"Do not let your hearts be troubled.
You believe in God; believe also in Me."

The Lord gives strength to His people;
the Lord blesses His people with peace.

Psalm 29:11

Put your hope in the Lord.
Travel steadily along His path.

Psalm 37:34

"I know the plans I have for you," declares
the LORD, "plans to prosper you and not to
harm you, plans to give you hope and a future."

Jeremiah 29:11

Your Word is a lamp to guide my feet
and a light for my path.

Psalm 119:105

"Do not be afraid; do not be discouraged, for the LORD
your God will be with you wherever you go."

Joshua 1:9

The LORD says, "I will guide you along the best pathway for your life. I will advise you and watch over you."

Psalm 32:8

Commit to the LORD whatever you do,
and He will establish your plans.

Proverbs 16:3

Whether you turn to the right or to the left,
your ears will hear a voice behind you, saying,
"This is the way; walk in it."

Isaiah 30:21

God said, "My Presence will go with you.
I'll see the journey to the end."

Exodus 33:14

God is our God for ever and ever;
He will be our Guide even to the end.

Psalm 48:14

God is our refuge and strength,
a very present help in trouble.

Psalm 46:1

Cast your cares on the Lᴏʀᴅ and He will sustain you.

Psalm 55:22

"Be still, and know that I am God."

The LORD is good, a refuge in times of trouble.
He cares for those who trust in Him.

Nahum 1:7

The Lord Himself goes before you and will be with you;
He will never leave you nor forsake you.

Deuteronomy 31:8

We have this hope as an anchor for the soul,
firm and secure.

Whoever dwells in the shelter of the Most High
will rest in the shadow of the Almighty.

Psalm 91:1

The eternal God is your refuge,
and underneath are the everlasting arms.

Deuteronomy 33:27

The LORD is my rock, my fortress and my deliverer;
my God is my rock, in whom I take refuge.

Psalm 18:2

I can do everything through Christ,
who gives me strength.

Philippians 4:13

The Lord will be your confidence and
will keep your foot from being caught.

Proverbs 3:26

Blessed is the one who trusts in the LORD,
whose confidence is in Him.

Jeremiah 17:7

Trust in the LORD forever, for the LORD God
is an everlasting rock.

Isaiah 26:4

"Do not let your hearts be troubled.
You believe in God; believe also in Me."

John 14:1

The LORD gives strength to His people;
the LORD blesses His people with peace.

Psalm 29:11

Put your hope in the LORD.
Travel steadily along His path.

Psalm 37:34

"I know the plans I have for you," declares
the LORD, "plans to prosper you and not to
harm you, plans to give you hope and a future."

Jeremiah 29:11

Your Word is a lamp to guide my feet
and a light for my path.

Psalm 119:105

"Do not be afraid; do not be discouraged, for the Lord
your God will be with you wherever you go."

Joshua 1:9

The LORD says, "I will guide you along the best pathway for your life. I will advise you and watch over you."

Psalm 32:8

Commit to the LORD whatever you do,
and He will establish your plans.

Proverbs 16:3

Whether you turn to the right or to the left,
your ears will hear a voice behind you, saying,
"This is the way; walk in it."

Isaiah 30:21

God said, "My Presence will go with you.
I'll see the journey to the end."

Exodus 33:14

God is our God for ever and ever;
He will be our Guide even to the end.

Psalm 48:14

God is our refuge and strength,
a very present help in trouble.

Psalm 46:1

Cast your cares on the LORD and He will sustain you.

Psalm 55:22

"Be still, and know that I am God."

Psalm 46:10

The Lord is good, a refuge in times of trouble.
He cares for those who trust in Him.

Nahum 1:7

The Lord Himself goes before you and will be with you;
He will never leave you nor forsake you.

We have this hope as an anchor for the soul,
firm and secure.

Whoever dwells in the shelter of the Most High
will rest in the shadow of the Almighty.

The eternal God is your refuge,
and underneath are the everlasting arms.

Deuteronomy 33:27

The Lᴏʀᴅ is my rock, my fortress and my deliverer;
my God is my rock, in whom I take refuge.

Psalm 18:2

I can do everything through Christ,
who gives me strength.

Philippians 4:13

The Lord will be your confidence and
will keep your foot from being caught.

Proverbs 3:26

Blessed is the one who trusts in the LORD,
whose confidence is in Him.

Jeremiah 17:7

Trust in the LORD forever, for the LORD God
is an everlasting rock.

Isaiah 26:4

"Do not let your hearts be troubled.
You believe in God; believe also in Me."

John 14:1

The Lord gives strength to His people;
the Lord blesses His people with peace.

Psalm 29:11

Put your hope in the LORD.
Travel steadily along His path.

Psalm 37:34

"I know the plans I have for you," declares
the LORD, "plans to prosper you and not to
harm you, plans to give you hope and a future."

Jeremiah 29:11

Your Word is a lamp to guide my feet
and a light for my path.

Psalm 119:105

"Do not be afraid; do not be discouraged, for the LORD
your God will be with you wherever you go."

Joshua 1:9

The Lord says, "I will guide you along the best pathway for your life. I will advise you and watch over you."

Psalm 32:8

Commit to the LORD whatever you do,
and He will establish your plans.

Proverbs 16:3

Whether you turn to the right or to the left,
your ears will hear a voice behind you, saying,
"This is the way; walk in it."

Isaiah 30:21

God said, "My Presence will go with you.
I'll see the journey to the end."

Exodus 33:14

God is our God for ever and ever;
He will be our Guide even to the end.

Psalm 48:14

God is our refuge and strength,
a very present help in trouble.

Psalm 46:1

Cast your cares on the LORD and He will sustain you.

Psalm 55:22

"Be still, and know that I am God."

Psalm 46:10

The LORD is good, a refuge in times of trouble.
He cares for those who trust in Him.

Nahum 1:7

The LORD Himself goes before you and will be with you;
He will never leave you nor forsake you.

Deuteronomy 31:8

We have this hope as an anchor for the soul,
firm and secure.

Hebrews 6:19

Whoever dwells in the shelter of the Most High
will rest in the shadow of the Almighty.

Psalm 91:1

The eternal God is your refuge,
and underneath are the everlasting arms.

Deuteronomy 33:27

The LORD is my rock, my fortress and my deliverer;
my God is my rock, in whom I take refuge.

Psalm 18:2

I can do everything through Christ,
who gives me strength.

The LORD will be your confidence and
will keep your foot from being caught.

Proverbs 3:26

Blessed is the one who trusts in the LORD,
whose confidence is in Him.

Jeremiah 17:7

Trust in the Lord forever, for the Lord God
is an everlasting rock.

Isaiah 26:4

"Do not let your hearts be troubled.
You believe in God; believe also in Me."

John 14:1

The LORD gives strength to His people;
the LORD blesses His people with peace.

Psalm 29:11

Put your hope in the LORD.
Travel steadily along His path.

Psalm 37:34

"I know the plans I have for you," declares
the LORD, "plans to prosper you and not to
harm you, plans to give you hope and a future."

Jeremiah 29:11

Your Word is a lamp to guide my feet
and a light for my path.

"Do not be afraid; do not be discouraged, for the LORD your God will be with you wherever you go."

Joshua 1:9

The Lord says, "I will guide you along the best pathway for your life. I will advise you and watch over you."

Commit to the Lᴏʀᴅ whatever you do,
and He will establish your plans.

Proverbs 16:3

Whether you turn to the right or to the left,
your ears will hear a voice behind you, saying,
"This is the way; walk in it."

Isaiah 30:21

God said, "My Presence will go with you.
I'll see the journey to the end."

God is our God for ever and ever;
He will be our Guide even to the end.

Psalm 48:14

God is our refuge and strength,
a very present help in trouble.

Psalm 46:1

Cast your cares on the L ORD and He will sustain you.

"Be still, and know that I am God."

Psalm 46:10

The Lord is good, a refuge in times of trouble.
He cares for those who trust in Him.

Nahum 1:7

The LORD Himself goes before you and will be with you;
He will never leave you nor forsake you.

Deuteronomy 31:8

We have this hope as an anchor for the soul,
firm and secure.

Hebrews 6:19

Whoever dwells in the shelter of the Most High
will rest in the shadow of the Almighty.

Psalm 91:1

The eternal God is your refuge,
and underneath are the everlasting arms.

Deuteronomy 33:27

The Lᴏʀᴅ is my rock, my fortress and my deliverer;
my God is my rock, in whom I take refuge.

I can do everything through Christ,
who gives me strength.

The LORD will be your confidence and
will keep your foot from being caught.

Proverbs 3:26

Blessed is the one who trusts in the LORD,
whose confidence is in Him.

Jeremiah 17:7

Trust in the Lord forever, for the Lord God
is an everlasting rock.

Isaiah 26:4

"Do not let your hearts be troubled.
You believe in God; believe also in Me."

John 14:1

The Lord gives strength to His people;
the Lord blesses His people with peace.

Psalm 29:11

Put your hope in the LORD.
Travel steadily along His path.

Psalm 37:34

"I know the plans I have for you," declares
the Lord, "plans to prosper you and not to
harm you, plans to give you hope and a future."

Jeremiah 29:11

Your Word is a lamp to guide my feet
and a light for my path.

Psalm 119:105

"Do not be afraid; do not be discouraged, for the LORD
your God will be with you wherever you go."

Joshua 1:9

The LORD says, "I will guide you along the best pathway for your life. I will advise you and watch over you."

Psalm 32:8

Commit to the Lord whatever you do,
and He will establish your plans.

Proverbs 16:3

Whether you turn to the right or to the left,
your ears will hear a voice behind you, saying,
"This is the way; walk in it."

Isaiah 30:21

God said, "My Presence will go with you.
I'll see the journey to the end."

Exodus 33:14

God is our God for ever and ever;
He will be our Guide even to the end.

Psalm 48:14

God is our refuge and strength,
a very present help in trouble.

Cast your cares on the Lᴏʀᴅ and He will sustain you.

Psalm 55:22

"Be still, and know that I am God."

Psalm 46:10

The Lord is good, a refuge in times of trouble.
He cares for those who trust in Him.

Nahum 1:7

The LORD Himself goes before you and will be with you;
He will never leave you nor forsake you.

Deuteronomy 31:8

We have this hope as an anchor for the soul,
firm and secure.

Hebrews 6:19

Whoever dwells in the shelter of the Most High
will rest in the shadow of the Almighty.

Psalm 91:1

The eternal God is your refuge,
and underneath are the everlasting arms.

Deuteronomy 33:27

The Lord is my rock, my fortress and my deliverer;
my God is my rock, in whom I take refuge.

Psalm 18:2

I can do everything through Christ,
who gives me strength.

The LORD will be your confidence and
will keep your foot from being caught.

Proverbs 3:26

Blessed is the one who trusts in the LORD,
whose confidence is in Him.

Jeremiah 17:7

Trust in the LORD forever, for the LORD God
is an everlasting rock.

Isaiah 26:4

"Do not let your hearts be troubled.
You believe in God; believe also in Me."

John 14:1

The LORD gives strength to His people;
the LORD blesses His people with peace.

Psalm 29:11

Put your hope in the LORD.
Travel steadily along His path.

Psalm 37:34

"I know the plans I have for you," declares
the LORD, "plans to prosper you and not to
harm you, plans to give you hope and a future."

Jeremiah 29:11

Your Word is a lamp to guide my feet
and a light for my path.

Psalm 119:105

"Do not be afraid; do not be discouraged, for the LORD your God will be with you wherever you go."

Joshua 1:9

The Lord says, "I will guide you along the best pathway for your life. I will advise you and watch over you."

Psalm 32:8

Commit to the LORD whatever you do,
and He will establish your plans.

Proverbs 16:3

Whether you turn to the right or to the left,
your ears will hear a voice behind you, saying,
"This is the way; walk in it."

Isaiah 30:21

God said, "My Presence will go with you.
I'll see the journey to the end."

Exodus 33:14

God is our God for ever and ever;
He will be our Guide even to the end.

Psalm 48:14

God is our refuge and strength,
a very present help in trouble.

Psalm 46:1

Kaiser · Psychiatry appointment
714-644-6480
O.C. Psychiatry

Che
1st intake evaluator
licensed therapist

1 1/2 hrs →
Anaheim -
★ Euclid wed this
Wed - 1:00pm
Holley Thao Thao 12:30
Trinh Co pay 20.00
1188 N. Euclid St.
Anaheim

Cast your cares on the LORD and He will sustain you.

Psalm 55:22